LAST

9/11 OX

1/11

CR

GREATEST HITS

By John Hamilton

Published by ABDO Publishing Company, 8000 West 78th Street, Suite 310, Edina, MN 55439. Copyright ©2011 by Abdo Consulting Group, Inc. International copyrights reserved in all countries. No part of this book may be reproduced in any form without written permission from the publisher. A&D Xtreme™ is a trademark and logo of ABDO Publishing Company.

Printed in the United States of America, North Mankato, Minnesota.
052010
092010

Editor: Sue Hamilton
Graphic Design: John Hamilton
Cover Photo: Getty Images
Interior Photos: AP Images, p. 2, 3, 12-13, 30-31; Corbis, p. 18, 23; Getty Images, p. 1, 4-5, 6-7, 8, 9, 10-11, 16, 17, 20, 21, 25 (bottom), 27 (bottom), 29 (bottom), 32; Ray Kasprowicz, p. 14-15, 19, 22, 24 (top & bottom), 25 (top), 26 (top & bottom), 27 (top), 28 (top & bottom), 29 (top).

Library of Congress Cataloging-in-Publication Data

Hamilton, John, 1959-
  Greatest hits / John Hamilton.
      p. cm. -- (Xtreme UFC)
  Includes index.
  ISBN 978-1-61613-474-7
  1. Mixed martial arts--Juvenile literature. 2. Ultimate Fighting Championship (Organization)--Juvenile literature. I. Title.
  GV1102.7.M59H36 2010
  796.815--dc22
                                    2010018785

CONTENTS

Which martial art is the best? That's the question the Ultimate Fighting Championship (UFC) organization tried to answer when it held its first tournament in 1993 in Denver, Colorado. Fighters from around the world competed to see which style would come out on top.

HISTORY

At UFC 1, on November 12, 1993, jiu-jitsu expert Royce Gracie, from Brazil, defeated boxer Art Jimmerson, from the United States. Gracie won the tournament.

Xtreme Fight

At UFC 1, martial artist Gerard Gordeau of Holland fought sumo wrestler Teila Tull of Hawaii. Gordeau won the match and advanced to the final, where he lost to Royce Gracie.

Xtreme Fight

Mixed Martial Arts

UFC 1 proved that a well-rounded fighter, a mixed martial artist, could beat someone skilled in only one style. Striking *and* ground fighting were both important. UFC events became very popular. By the mid-1990s, millions of people had become fans of this new contact sport.

By 1997, many people wanted to ban UFC tournaments. They thought mixed martial arts events were too violent. In the early days of the sport, there were few rules. "No-holds-barred" fighting meant severe injuries could occur. Many states and TV cable companies banned UFC events.

CONTROVERSY

Senator John McCain of Arizona once compared mixed martial arts to "human cockfighting," a form of animal abuse. He called on all the states to ban the new sport.

Xtreme Fact

In the late 1990s, the UFC added new rules. Some attacks, such as biting, hair pulling, or groin strikes, were banned. Weight classes and timed rounds were added to make the fights more fair. Referees and judges became more important. These and other changes made mixed martial arts more acceptable to the public.

REFORM

Junior dos Santos (top) battled Gabriel Gonzaga during a heavyweight match at UFC Fight Night, March 21, 2010. Referee Josh Rosenthal supervised the action.

GOING

In 2001, the UFC changed management. A company called Zuffa became the new owner. Fight manager Dana White became the new president. White was determined to make the UFC more popular. After additional rule changes, UFC events spread to more states and pay-per-view cable TV channels. By the late 2000s, mixed martial arts became one of the fastest-growing sports in the United States.

Dana White

MAINSTREAM

At UFC 67, on February 3, 2007, Croatian fighter Mirko Cro Cop faced American mixed martial artist Eddie Sanchez. Cro Cop beat Sanchez in the first round.

Xtreme Fight

The Ultimate Fighter

In 2005, Spike TV began airing *The Ultimate Fighter (TUF)*. The reality series featured a group of mixed martial artists competing in the Octagon for a spot in the UFC. The show was an immediate hit, and launched the careers of several UFC fighters.

Xtreme Fight

At the end of season 8 of *The Ultimate Fighter*, on December 14, 2008, Efrain Escudero (bottom) defeated Phillipe Nover in three rounds in a unanimous decision.

The Gracie family, from Brazil, founded Brazilian jiu-jitsu. It was based on a martial art from Japan. The Gracies often held *vale tudo* events. These were no-holds-barred mixed martial arts competitions. Together with associates from the United States, they formed the Ultimate Fighting Championship. Famous Gracie family members include Rorion, Rolls, Hélio, and Royce, seen here entering the arena at a mixed martial arts event.

LEGENDS

On November 12, 1993, UFC Hall of Famer Royce Gracie won UFC 1 in Denver, Colorado. Royce was also victorious at the UFC 2 and UFC 4 tournaments.

KEN SHAMROCK

- UFC Hall of Fame
- UFC Superfight Champion
- Style: Catch Wrestling, Shootfighting
- Nickname: The World's Most Dangerous Man

MARK COLEMAN

- UFC Hall of Fame
- UFC Heavyweight Champion
- Style: Freestyle Wrestling
- Nickname: The Hammer

RANDY COUTURE

- UFC Hall of Fame
- UFC Heavyweight, Light Heavyweight Champion
- Style: Greco-Roman Wrestling, Boxing
- Nickname: The Natural

CHUCK LIDDELL

- UFC Hall of Fame
- UFC Light Heavyweight Champion
- Style: Karate, Kickboxing, Brazilian Jiu-Jitsu
- Nickname: The Iceman

MATT HUGHES

- UFC Hall of Fame
- UFC Welterweight Champion
- Style: Wrestling, Boxing

TITO ORTIZ

- UFC Light Heavyweight Champion
- Style: Wrestling, Boxing
- Nickname: The Huntington Beach Bad Boy

BROCK LESNAR

- UFC Heavyweight Champion
- Style: Wrestling, Boxing

WANDERLEI SILVA

- Pride Middleweight Champion (Japan)
- Style: Muay Thai, Brazilian Jiu-Jitsu

FRANK MIR

- UFC Heavyweight Champion
- Style: Karate, Jiu-Jitsu

QUINTON JACKSON

- UFC Light Heavyweight Champion
- Style: Wrestling, Boxing

LYOTO MACHIDA

- UFC Light Heavyweight Champion
- Style: Karate, Jiu-Jitsu

FRANKIE EDGAR

- UFC Lightweight Champion
- Style: Wrestling, Boxing, Jiu-Jitsu

RASHAD EVANS

- UFC Light Heavyweight Champion
- Style: Wrestling, Boxing, Jiu-Jitsu

RICH FRANKLIN

- UFC Middleweight Champion
- Style: Kickboxing, Jiu-Jitsu

GEORGES ST-PIERRE

- UFC Welterweight Champion
- Style: Karate, Jiu-Jitsu

FORREST GRIFFIN

- UFC Light Heavyweight Champion
- Style: Kickboxing, Jiu-Jitsu

BJ PENN

- UFC Lightweight, Welterweight Champion
- Style: Jiu-Jitsu, Boxing

ANDERSON SILVA

- UFC Middleweight Champion
- Style: Tae Kwon Do, Jiu-Jitsu, Judo

Brazilian Jiu-Jitsu

A fighting style made popular by fighters from Brazil that specializes in grappling and ground fighting, including chokes and joint locks.

Decision

If a match finishes without a clear victor, either by knockout or submission, a panel of three judges decides the winner. If only two judges agree on the winner, it is called a split decision.

Greco-Roman Wrestling

A style of wrestling commonly used in Olympic Games competition. Holds below the waist are forbidden. Throws and headlocks are important.

Kickboxing

A style of fighting that relies mainly on a mix of kicking and punching. Muay Thai is a type of kickboxing that is the national sport of Thailand.

GLOSSARY

Mixed Martial Arts
A full-contact sport that allows a mix of different martial arts, such as boxing, karate, and wrestling. The most popular mixed martial arts (MMA) organization is the Ultimate Fighting Championship (UFC).

Octagon
The eight-sided ring in which Ultimate Fighting Championship fighters compete.

Shootfighting
A style of fighting that combines several types of martial arts, including Muay Thai kickboxing and wrestling.

Tae Kwon Do
A martial art that is the national sport of South Korea. Tae Kwon Do emphasizes powerful strikes, especially high, leaping kicks.

INDEX